GLIMMERS JOURNAL

REFLECT ON

THE SMALL MOMENTS

THAT BRING YOU JOY,

SAFETY, AND CONNECTION

GLIMMERS JOURNAL

DEB DANA

W. W. NORTON & COMPANY

Independent Publishers Since 1923

Important Note: *Glimmers Journal* is intended to provide general information on the subject of health and well-being; it is not a substitute for medical or psychological treatment and may not be relied upon for purposes of diagnosing or treating any illness. Please seek out the care of a professional healthcare provider if you are pregnant, nursing, or experiencing symptoms of any potentially serious condition.

Any URLs displayed in this book link or refer to websites that existed as of press time. The publisher is not responsible for, and should not be deemed to endorse or recommend, any website other than its own or any content that it did not create. The author, also, is not responsible for any third-party material.

For information about permission to reproduce selections from this book, write to Permissions, W. W. Norton & Company, Inc., 500 Fifth Avenue, New York, NY 10110

For information about special discounts for bulk purchases, please contact W. W. Norton Special Sales at specialsales@wwnorton.com or 800-233-4830

Manufacturing through Asia Pacific
Book design by Lauren Graessle
Production managers: Gwen Cullen/Ramona Wilkes

ISBN: 978-1-324-08207-1

W. W. Norton & Company, Inc., 500 Fifth Avenue, New York, NY 10110
www.wwnorton.com

W. W. Norton & Company Ltd., 15 Carlisle Street, London W1D 3BS

1 2 3 4 5 6 7 8 9 0

TO EVERYONE JOINING ME ON THIS JOURNEY.
SENDING A GLIMMER TO LIGHT YOUR WAY . . .

INTRODUCTION

The Power and Promise of Glimmers

Aglimmer of hope. A glimmer of light. The sky glimmering with stars. When you hear the word *glimmer*, where does it take you? My glimmer journey began with my work with clients who, even though their lives were filled with suffering, regularly found small moments of feeling safe and regulated enough to be present in their lives and find their way to connection. I began using the word *glimmer* to describe these times when, for just an instant, they felt a spark of joy. Since that clinical beginning, glimmers have moved beyond the therapy world and found their way into the imaginations of curious humans everywhere.

Through the lens of Polyvagal Theory, glimmers are micromoments of regulation that foster feelings of well-being. (If you are new to Polyvagal Theory or want to review the basics, you'll find a brief description of the three organizing principles of Polyvagal Theory and "The Beginner's Guide to Polyvagal Theory" at the end of the journal.) When we notice and name these glimmers, we shape our system toward regulation. I found that introducing the concept of glimmers to my clients created a path they could follow to increase their ability for regulation and connection and build a foundation for safely working with their experiences of trauma. It's important to understand that glimmers are not a form of toxic positivity. They are not a way to always look on the bright side or count your blessings and discount your suffering. They don't neutralize triggers. Recognizing glimmers doesn't minimize your distress or disavow the ways you are suffering. What they are is a reminder that the nervous system is exquisitely able to hold both dysregulation and regulation. Your days can be filled with difficulty, and you can also feel a spark of safety, regulation, and connection. This amazing capacity is built into your human biology.

Glimmers routinely appear in everyday life, yet frequently go unnoticed. A glimmer could be as simple as seeing a friendly face, hearing a soothing sound, or noticing something in the environment that brings a smile. They are personal to each of us, and one person's glimmer may be another person's trigger. Glimmers are a cue in the day, either internal or external, that sparks a sense of well-being. These tiny moments gently yet significantly shape your system toward well-being. They help you become regulated and ready for connection. Glimmers are easily overlooked because, to help you survive, the human brain is wired to pay more attention to negative events than positive ones. A micromoment of safety may make its way into awareness for a fleeting moment and then quickly disappear. Once you learn to look for glimmers, you find they are all around, you pay more attention to them, and you naturally begin to look for more. Glimmers are a reminder that ventral energy is always there waiting to be noticed and to nourish your nervous system.

The power of glimmers is that they are not a one-and-done experience. They accumulate and move you along the path toward physical and psychological well-being. You feel something shift. You feel a tiny change in your body. You notice a thought that holds a hint of hope. Your nervous system gathers glimmers, adding them up one by one until something in your world feels just a bit different. Keeping track of glimmers in an intentional way enhances this process. The *Glimmers Journal* is designed to give you a way to notice and name your glimmers—to stop and feel the spark of joy a glimmer brings.

HOW TO USE YOUR JOURNAL

The *Glimmers Journal* is designed to help you become aware of the people, places, and events that bring you glimmers and bring focused attention to those experiences. Most of us go through our days surrounded by glimmers without noticing them. The *Glimmers Journal* will help you notice, name, and be nourished by those sparks of regulating energy.

Categories help us organize our experience. When we sort things into groups, it is easier to acknowledge, arrange, and appreciate moments that otherwise may pass by without awareness. The *Glimmers Journal* uses five categories to support you on your glimmer journey: glimmers in nature, with people and animals, in art and science, embodied glimmers, and flavors of glimmers. Each category includes examples and suggestions to help you find glimmers and space for you to write about the glimmers you discover. The glimmer categories are followed by three additional sections: finding your glimmer environments, sharing your glimmers, and the practice of glimmering. These invite you to look beyond individual moments toward an expanded glimmer experience.

One of the mottoes of working with the nervous system is that there is no right or wrong way—just the way of your nervous system. Each nervous system finds its own path. Another motto is the phrase *in this moment*, recognizing that the nervous system is finding its way moment to moment, and what nourishes us doesn't necessarily remain constant. Honoring those two principles, there are many different ways to use your journal. You may want to go through the journal from start to finish, exploring one category at a time. Or you might decide to choose a different category each day and intentionally look for a glimmer in that category. Other times, you might just want to see what kinds of glimmers appear, and let yourself be surprised. You can keep your journal handy and add to it when you find a glimmer or reflect at the end of the day and look for glimmers that were on your path and enter them in your journal. Follow the wisdom of your nervous system as you turn to your journal and ask yourself how you want your glimmer journey to unfold.

THE BASIC GLIMMER
PRACTICE

Glimmers remind us that our nervous system knows the way to regulation and that when we build a practice of noticing the tiny moments, we find them more easily and see them more frequently. The six steps of the Basic Glimmer Practice give you a framework to become skillful at recognizing glimmers and to create a habit of tuning in to them.

● SEE

What are the cues that you have found a glimmer? What happens in your body that lets you know you are in a glimmer moment? What do you do when you feel that spark of energy? What thoughts arise? What emotions do you feel?

Find your cues.

● STOP

Now that you know the cues, use them to notice glimmers as you move through your day. Glimmers happen regularly, but because they are micro-moments, you need to be on the lookout for them. Look for predictable glimmer moments in specific places, with particular people, at certain times. Find the ways glimmers routinely appear. Be open to the unpredictable glimmers that may also appear. When you recognize one of the cues you identified, stop and find the glimmer.

What are some glimmers you found?

● **APPRECIATE**

Spend several seconds in appreciation letting the glimmer land in your system. Notice all the different feelings your glimmers bring. Create an easy way to acknowledge a glimmer as it happens. You might repeat a simple phrase or make a small movement (perhaps your hand on your heart or a finger pointing toward the glimmer) each time you find a glimmer. What are some ways you acknowledge a glimmer?

● **REMEMBER**

Find ways to track your glimmers. The *Glimmers Journal* is designed for this purpose and will give you a framework to track glimmers. In addition to your journal work, you could also write glimmer stories or poems, illustrate glimmers, or create glimmer photo collages or glimmer songs. Experiment with ways to build your collection and create a personal glimmer library. *What are you drawn to?*

● **SHARE**

When you share your glimmers with someone else, they come alive again in the remembering and retelling. You might text your glimmers to a friend or make talking about daily glimmers a family ritual. You could find a glimmer buddy or create a glimmer group. *You'll spend more time exploring this later in the journal, but for now, what is a way you want to share your glimmers?*

● **INTEND**

Setting an intention is a time-honored practice to support making a change and staying connected to a goal. Writing an autonomically informed intention involves bringing your brain-based intelligence and your nervous system–based wisdom together. Your brain and nervous system need to be on the same page. When your brain and body are not in agreement about the pathway to change, you'll struggle to realize an intention. Set an intention that brings the right degree of challenge—too bland and you'll lose interest; too big and you'll feel overwhelmed.

The right intention will catch, and keep, your interest.
Writing an intention involves a few steps. Find the words that feel like an invitation and not a demand—a possibility and not an expectation. Write them down and then read them, first to yourself and then out loud. Often as we write and then read our words, we find they don't land quite in the way we expected and need to make small changes. The intention I've discovered works for me is, "I am ready to see the glimmers that appear on my path today."

Now it's your turn to write a glimmer intention. Remember, you can revise your intention anytime you want. You might decide to write a new intention to begin each week, or write a couple of intentions and take turns using them, or you may find one intention that captures just what you are looking for.

WRITE A GLIMMER INTENTION, OR INTENTIONS,
TO BEGIN YOUR *GLIMMERS JOURNAL* JOURNEY.

GLIMMER CATEGORIES

With a general understanding of what glimmers are and how they work, let's move to a more specific exploration by diving into glimmer categories. We automatically, and often unconsciously, categorize things as a way to understand and interact with them. Intentionally using categories to group our glimmers brings patterns into awareness and helps us catch the glimmer moments.

GLIMMERS IN NATURE

BETWEEN EVERY TWO PINE TREES THERE IS
A DOOR LEADING TO A NEW WAY OF LIFE.

— JOHN MUIR

Our nervous systems are nurtured in nature. Moments in nature predictably reduce stress. The sights, sounds, and scents of nature are regulating, and when we are cut off from the natural world, we feel the disruption. Connecting with nature, even for a micromoment, is a restorative experience.

LOOK UP AT THE NIGHT SKY

For millennia, humans have been looking up into the night sky. We are stargazers. Whether looking out a window or standing under the stars, we are naturally drawn to search the sky.

LOOK FOR THE BIG DIPPER.

SEARCH FOR THE NORTH STAR.

MAKE A WISH ON A STAR.

FIND THE MOON.

DISCOVER PAINTINGS THAT BRING THE

NIGHT SKY ALIVE FOR YOU.

(Van Gogh's *Starry Night* is one of the most

famous paintings of the night sky.)

EXPLORE THE STARGAZING GLIMMERS THAT ARE

UNIQUELY YOURS . . .

TURN YOUR FACE
TOWARD THE SKY

Sky gazing is an invitation to stop focusing on what is in front of you and take a moment to look up instead. You can step out of the rush of the day to see the beauty that is above you.

LOOK FOR A DAYTIME MOON.

SAVOR THE SUNRISE.

SOAK IN THE SUNSET.

SEE ALL THE COLORS IN THE SKY.

FEEL THE SUN ON YOUR FACE.

FIND YOUR OWN SKY GAZING GLIMMERS . . .

EXPLORE THE CLOUDS

While clouds are useful in predicting weather, they also grab our imagination, taking us to a world beyond weather patterns. We're captivated by the changing shapes and colors as clouds move across the sky. We see pictures in clouds—faces, animals, familiar objects. This human ability to see meaningful images in a random pattern is called pareidolia, and studies suggest it enhances creativity.

FIND AN ANIMAL, FACE, OR OBJECT IN THE CLOUDS.

CREATE A CLOUD STORY.

LOOK FOR ALL THE DIFFERENT KINDS
AND COLORS OF CLOUDS.

TAKE IN A CLOUDSCAPE (A LARGE
FORMATION OF CLOUDS).

DELIGHT IN THE RAYS OF LIGHT
SHINING THROUGH THE CLOUDS.

DISCOVER YOUR CLOUD GLIMMERS . . .

TOUCH THE EARTH

Directly connecting to the earth, sometimes called earthing or grounding, helps regulate our physiology. We benefit from connection to the earth's natural electric charge.

WALK BAREFOOT.

DIG IN THE DIRT.

PUT YOUR HANDS IN THE SAND.

TOUCH THE GRASS.

UNEARTH YOUR GLIMMERS . . .

LISTEN FOR THE SOUNDS OF NATURE

Nature is never silent. There is a soundscape happening every moment, with birdsong, animal noises, the sounds of the wind and rain. While noise (unwanted, unpleasant sound) brings autonomic distress, the sounds of nature can reduce anxiety and increase regulation.

HEAR BIRDS SINGING.

LISTEN FOR ANIMALS TALKING.

CATCH THE SOUND OF THE WIND BLOWING
AND THE LEAVES RUSTLING.

TUNE IN TO THE SOUNDS OF WATER MOVING.

SEARCH FOR NATURE SOUNDS ONLINE.

GATHER THE NATURE SOUNDS THAT BRING
YOU GLIMMERS . . .

SEE THE WORLD IN COLOR

Beautiful sunsets, sparkling water, blue skies, and green forests are just some of the ways color can bring us a moment of joy. The colors in the natural world delight us, surprise us, and can amaze us.

FIND DIFFERENT SHADES OF A COLOR
IN THE WORLD AROUND YOU.
LOOK FOR A RAINBOW AFTER A STORM.
SEE THE GEOGRAPHY AROUND YOU
AS A COLOR PALETTE.
NOTICE THE DIFFERENT TINTS OF COLOR IN THE SKY.

DISCOVER THE COLORFUL GLIMMERS IN THE WORLD
AROUND YOU . . .

BEFRIEND A TREE

Throughout history, we have worshipped trees. Whether we imagine trees as keepers of ancient wisdom or mythologize them, simply sitting by a tree can bring the nervous system a moment of regulation.

TOUCH A TREE.

GATHER TREE LEAVES.

TAKE SHELTER UNDER A TREE.

COLLECT TREE PHOTOS.

DISCOVER YOUR TREE-INSPIRED GLIMMERS . . .

WATCH A CREATURE FLY

Birds, butterflies, and bugs hover, flit, glide, soar, flutter, take off, and land in amazing ways. We often see spiritual meaning in birds soaring above us, messages in butterflies appearing, and symbolism with certain insects. We are intrigued watching a creature in flight. Anxiety goes down. Regulation and a sense of connection go up.

LOOK FOR BIRDS, BUTTERFLIES, AND BUGS IN
FLIGHT AS YOU GO THROUGH YOUR DAY.
FIND THE BIRDS THAT SHARE YOUR ENVIRONMENT.
FOLLOW THE FLIGHT OF A BIRD, BUTTERFLY, OR
BUG, AND FEEL YOURSELF FLYING WITH THEM.
CREATE A COLLECTION OF PHOTOS
OF CREATURES IN FLIGHT.

LET YOUR GLIMMERS TAKE FLIGHT . . .

SOAK IN THE SCENTS OF NATURE

Scent is a significant nervous system regulator, and the smells of nature have been shown to be particularly nourishing as they are often linked to certain places and personal memories. The smell of earth after a rainstorm, salty ocean air, flowers in bloom, and freshly cut grass are just some examples of the ways nature scents can rekindle a memory and bring a moment of joy.

STEP OUTSIDE AND TAKE IN ALL
THE SCENTS AROUND YOU.
CREATE A LIST OF SCENTS YOU LIKE.
TRACE AN ENJOYABLE NATURE SCENT
BACK TO A MEMORY AND SAVOR IT.
GO FOR A WALK AND SEE WHAT
SCENTS FEEL INVITING.
WHEN YOU FIND A SCENT YOU LOVE, STOP, TAKE IN
THE ENVIRONMENT, AND MAKE A NEW MEMORY.

FIND THE FRAGRANCES OF YOUR GLIMMERS . . .

FIND A MOMENT OF PLAY

Nature is a natural playground. Moments of play bring moments of regulation, and each time we venture outside, we have an opportunity to be playful.

DANCE IN THE RAIN.

SPLASH IN A PUDDLE.

CATCH A SNOWFLAKE ON YOUR TONGUE.

CLIMB A BOULDER.

BALANCE ON A LOG.

HEAD OUTSIDE AND FIND YOUR
PLAY-FILLED GLIMMERS . . .

OTHER GLIMMERS IN NATURE
THAT NOURISH ME

THE PEOPLE (AND ANIMALS) IN OUR LIVES

WHILE LONELINESS HAS THE POTENTIAL TO KILL, CONNECTION HAS EVEN MORE POTENTIAL TO HEAL.

— VIVEK MURTHY

We are wired for connection. We find regulation in relationship with others. How connected or lonely we feel impacts both our physical and emotional health. Finding moments of safe connection, and having a variety of different kinds of connections, is a necessary ingredient for well-being. Every day, we long for, and look for, opportunities to co-regulate by reaching out to the people, and animals, in the world around us.

LOOK FOR SIMPLE CONNECTIONS

Sometimes a quick connection that doesn't require a big commitment is just what we need to be reminded that we belong. When we connect with people during the regular social interactions that happen as we move through our days, we feel welcome in the world.

SMILE AT A STRANGER.

HOLD A DOOR OPEN FOR SOMEONE.

SAY HELLO TO SOMEONE PASSING BY.

TALK WITH SOMEONE STANDING IN LINE WITH YOU.

FIND YOUR SIMPLE GLIMMERS . . .

RENEW OLD FRIENDSHIPS

Reconnecting with old friends can be surprisingly nourishing. The person we reach out to feels touched by being remembered, and we feel the happiness of recovering a lost connection.

REACH OUT TO SOMEONE YOU'VE LOST TOUCH WITH.

SEND A MESSAGE TO A CHILDHOOD FRIEND.

FIND OUT WHAT OLD FRIENDS ARE DOING NOW.

REMEMBER AN OLD FRIEND AND A

MOMENT OF FUN YOU HAD.

REDISCOVER GLIMMERS . . .

STAY CONNECTED

Reliable friendships nourish our nervous systems. Maintaining regular connection is an important part of being a good friend.

TEXT, PHONE, OR WRITE TO A FRIEND.

PLAN A GET-TOGETHER.

MEET A FRIEND FOR COFFEE.

CREATE A NEW MEMORY.

FIND THE GLIMMERS IN YOUR RELIABLE
CONNECTIONS . . .

REACH FOR RECIPROCITY

Reciprocity is a connection between people that is created in the back-and-forth communication between autonomic nervous systems. We are nourished in experiences of reciprocity, feeling the ebb and flow of giving and receiving.

ENJOY THE RHYTHM THAT HAPPENS IN
CONVERSATION AS YOU TALK AND LISTEN.
TAKE TURNS PLANNING ACTIVITIES.
PRACTICE OFFERING TO HELP AND ASKING FOR HELP.
JOIN A GROUP THAT SHARES ONE OF YOUR
INTERESTS AND SEE WHERE IT TAKES YOU.
CULTIVATE GRATITUDE—RECEIVING A KINDNESS
AND OFFERING ONE IN RETURN.

LOOK FOR GLIMMERS IN THE EBB AND
FLOW OF CONNECTION . . .

RELIVE AND REMEMBER

Reminiscing is a pathway to regulation. When we remember moments that were glimmer-filled, we return to them and feel them come alive again.

CREATE A PHOTO COLLAGE OF PEOPLE WHO
BRING YOU JOY.

SHARE A MEMORY WITH A FRIEND.

RETURN TO A SPECIAL PLACE.

START A FAMILY AND FRIENDS MEMORY BOOK.

COLLECT YOUR GLIMMER MEMORIES . . .

CREATE COMMUNITY

Nervous system to nervous system, we are connected to others in ways that can feel magical and even miraculous. We connect with one another not just for individual well-being but for the well-being of our human family. We gather people, welcome them in, and engage with them with joy, for fun, and with purpose.

GO TO A COMMUNITY EVENT.

NOTICE THE DIFFERENT PEOPLE THAT

MAKE UP YOUR COMMUNITIES.

BECOME AWARE OF THE WAYS YOU

ARE HELD IN COMMUNITY.

INVITE PEOPLE INTO YOUR CIRCLES OF CONNECTION.

SAVOR THE DIFFERENT WAYS

CONNECTIONS NOURISH YOU.

REACH OUT AND FIND COMMUNITY GLIMMERS . . .

FIND FRIENDLY TOUCH

Touch can be a powerful regulator of our nervous systems. It can reduce anxiety and help us feel anchored in safety. Finding warm, friendly, non-sexual touch that feels welcome is a pathway to connection.

HOLD HANDS.

SIT SIDE BY SIDE, SHOULDERS TOUCHING.

REST YOUR HEAD ON SOMEONE'S SHOULDER.

GIVE A HUG — GET A HUG.

TOUCH INTO YOUR GLIMMERS . . .

CONNECT WITH
ANIMAL FRIENDS

Human–animal relationships have the potential to shape our systems toward physical and emotional well-being. We cherish our pets and the relationships we have with them. They become part of our family, helping us stay physically active and emotionally regulated. Encountering people walking their dogs, being with horses, seeing sheep and goats in fields and wild animals in their natural environments are moments of connection that surprise and delight us.

SNUGGLE A PET.

FIND A PICTURE OF AN ANIMAL THAT BRINGS A
SMILE, OR WATCH FUNNY ANIMAL VIDEOS.

PET-SIT FOR A FRIEND OR VOLUNTEER AT A SHELTER.

TAKE A WALK AND GREET THE DOGS AND THEIR
HUMANS YOU MEET ALONG THE WAY.

GO ON A NATURE WALK AND SEE WHAT ANIMALS
INHABIT THE WORLD AROUND YOU.

DISCOVER THE GLIMMERS THAT WAIT FOR YOU IN THE
ANIMAL WORLD . . .

MORE GLIMMERS IN CONNECTION

SCIENCE AND ART

THE ARTS AND SCIENCES ARE AVATARS OF
HUMAN CREATIVITY.

— MAE JEMISON

Science and art may seem like an odd pairing, but they are both pathways to understanding and describing our world. We experiment with science and explore with art. Science is often an act of creativity, and creating art often relies on scientific knowledge. Each takes us on a journey of discovery, helping us see the world in a new way. Fractals are a wonderful example of the integration of science and art. A fractal is a mathematical shape that forms a visual pattern that repeats over and over. They are easily found in nature, in works of art, and in computer-generated images (e.g., a nautilus shell, snowflakes, romanesco broccoli, Jackson Pollock paintings), and looking at a fractal for just a few seconds helps regulate our nervous systems.

GET A TASTE OF SCIENCE

Science shapes our world, and while for many of us the idea of diving into rigorous scientific study is not something that feels doable or even desirable, we can all dip a toe into the world of science.

JOIN A SCIENCE EMAIL LIST AND GET A SCIENCE
FACT DELIVERED TO YOUR INBOX DAILY.
APPRECIATE ALL THE WAYS SCIENTIFIC DISCOVERIES
INCREASE THE QUALITY OF YOUR LIFE.
WATCH A MOVIE ABOUT SCIENTISTS
(E.G., *RADIOACTIVE, HIDDEN FIGURES,*
A BEAUTIFUL MIND, THE THEORY OF EVERYTHING,
THE MAN WHO KNEW INFINITY).
LOOK AT IMAGES FROM NASA AND
THE HUBBLE TELESCOPE.
FIND FRACTALS.

DIP A TOE INTO SCIENCE AND SEE WHAT GLIMMERS
YOU FIND . . .

EMBRACE TECHNOLOGY

While some forms of technology are disconnecting and dysregulating, others make life a bit easier and bring us together. Technology can improve the quality of our human experience. When we reach for technology that brings joy, ease, and connection, we are reaching for regulation.

CELEBRATE TECHNOLOGY SUCCESS — A MOMENT WHEN YOU SUCCESSFULLY NAVIGATE A NEW PIECE OF TECHNOLOGY OR DISCOVER A NEW FUNCTION OF A DEVICE.

DOWNLOAD AN APP THAT HELPS YOU FIND YOUR WAY TO REGULATION.

SAMPLE A PODCAST OR LISTEN TO AN AUDIOBOOK.

CREATE A GLIMMER SLIDESHOW.

USE TECHNOLOGY TO STAY CONNECTED WITH SOMEONE WHO IS FAR AWAY.

EMBRACE TECHNOLOGY AND FIND YOUR GLIMMERS . . .

SEE THE PATTERNS IN YOUR ENVIRONMENT

As we move through the day, we are surrounded by shapes and colors that organically impact our nervous systems and have the power to move us toward regulation.

SEE THE DIFFERENT SHAPES IN YOUR ENVIRONMENT —
SPIRALS, CURVES, ANGLES, STRAIGHT LINES.
REORGANIZE A SPACE. SEE WHAT DELIGHTS
YOU IN THE NEW ARRANGEMENT.
NOTICE THE COLORS IN THE SPACES YOU INHABIT.
ADD A SPLASH OF COLOR TO YOUR ENVIRONMENT.

EXPLORE THE PATTERNS IN YOUR SPACES AND FIND
YOUR GLIMMERS . . .

EXPLORE THE WORLD OF ART

Connection with art, whether we make it ourselves or appreciate what other people have created, is a pathway to regulation.

VISIT AN ART GALLERY OR GO TO AN ART FAIR.

CONNECT WITH A LOCAL ARTIST.

TAKE PHOTOS THAT BRING YOU A SENSE OF JOY.

COLLECT IMAGES THAT FILL YOU WITH WONDER.

EXPERIMENT WITH CREATING SOMETHING.

BRING YOUR CREATIVE GLIMMERS TO LIFE . . .

INVITE MUSIC IN

Music is abundant in our everyday lives. It accompanies us as we move through the day, which makes it easy to turn to for a quick moment of joy.

LISTEN DURING YOUR DAY FOR MUSIC THAT
BRINGS A SMILE.

NOTICE THE SONGS YOU HUM OR SING ALONG TO.

FIND THE SONGS THAT MAKE YOU WANT TO DANCE.

CREATE A GLIMMER PLAYLIST.

LISTEN FOR YOUR MUSICAL GLIMMERS . . .

FURTHER EXPLORATION OF MY SCIENCE AND ART GLIMMERS

EMBODIED GLIMMERS

THE BODY SAYS WHAT WORDS CANNOT.
— MARTHA GRAHAM

We experience moments of safety and connection not just as thoughts or feelings. We also feel them in our bodies. Eighty percent of our vagal fibers send information from the body to the brain, and when we are disconnected from our embodied experience we are also cut off from the wisdom of our nervous system. Accessing this somatic circuitry shapes our experience of being human. When we tune in to the feeling of a glimmer in our bodies, we feel the physical expression of the experience that is then sent to our brains and translated into a story.

MOVE

Movement is an essential ingredient in our physical and emotional well-being. While regular exercise is important for overall health, small moments of movement delight us and nourish us in other important ways.

JUMP FOR JOY!

MOVE IN A WAY THAT MAKES YOU HAPPY.

DANCE.

STRETCH YOUR ARMS OUT WIDE AND HUG THE WORLD.

REACH FOR THE SKY.

EXPERIENCE YOUR GLIMMERS IN MOTION . . .

BREATHE

Breath is an autonomic activity and has a direct connection to the autonomic nervous system. The way we breathe can quickly bring a moment of regulation and connection.

EXHALE DEEPLY.

PLAY WITH BREATH PRACTICES THAT

FILL YOU WITH ENERGY.

BLOW BUBBLES.

TRY RESISTANCE BREATHING — PRETEND YOU

ARE BLOWING THROUGH A STRAW.

SIGH WITH CONTENTMENT.

FOLLOW YOUR BREATH AND FIND YOUR GLIMMERS . . .

MAKE A JOYFUL NOISE

We express ourselves through sound. Some sounds make music, some tell a story without words, and others turn into language. And each of them can bring the feeling of a glimmer to life.

LAUGH OUT LOUD.

PLAY A KAZOO.

WHISTLE.

MAKE A SOUND THAT COMMUNICATES

THE FEELING OF A GLIMMER.

WRITE A LIST OF WORDS THAT MAKE YOU SMILE

AND WEAVE THEM INTO YOUR CONVERSATIONS.

LISTEN FOR THE SOUNDS OF YOUR GLIMMERS . . .

CELEBRATE

When we celebrate an embodied glimmer moment, we are inviting our brain to partner with our nervous system and mark the moment to deepen its impact.

APPRECIATE A MOMENT WHEN YOUR BODY
SUPPORTS YOU.

DO SOMETHING YOU LOVE.

EAT YOUR FAVORITE FOOD.

FIND THE WORDS THAT BRING YOUR
CELEBRATION ALIVE. YAHOO!

CELEBRATE YOUR GLIMMERS . . .

DEEPER INTO EMBODIED GLIMMERS

FLAVORS OF GLIMMERS

VARIETY IS THE SOUL OF PLEASURE.

— APHRA BEHN

Glimmers carry the full range of feelings that are possible when we are regulated. More than just moments of feeling happy or at peace, glimmers include everything from feeling calm to joyful, purposeful to playful, relaxed to excited. We can think about these different feelings as flavors of glimmers. When we discover the variety of flavors available to us, they become even easier to find.

FIND YOUR FLAVORS

While many glimmer flavors and feelings are shared, we each have our own favorites and words to describe them.

MAKE A LIST OF GLIMMER FLAVORS. WHEN YOU
FIND A NEW ONE, ADD IT TO YOUR LIST.
WHAT'S YOUR FAVORITE FLAVOR?
WHAT FLAVOR DO YOU FIND MOST OFTEN,
AND WHAT ONE IS MOST ELUSIVE?
CHOOSE A FLAVOR OF THE DAY AND LOOK FOR IT.
SEE HOW MANY DIFFERENT FLAVORS
YOU FIND IN A DAY OR A WEEK.

FIND YOUR GLIMMER FLAVORS . . .

BE OPEN TO THE UNEXPECTED

Glimmers can appear at times and in places we don't expect to find them. The unpredictable ones surprise us and are a reminder that we never know when a glimmer might appear.

RUN INTO AN OLD FRIEND.

CONNECT UNEXPECTEDLY WITH A LOVED ONE.

FIND A LUCKY PENNY ON THE STREET.

BE SURPRISED WHEN A STRANGER OFFERS

A KINDNESS. PAY IT FORWARD!

RECEIVE AN UNEXPECTED THANK YOU.

DISCOVER GLIMMERS THAT SURPRISE YOU . . .

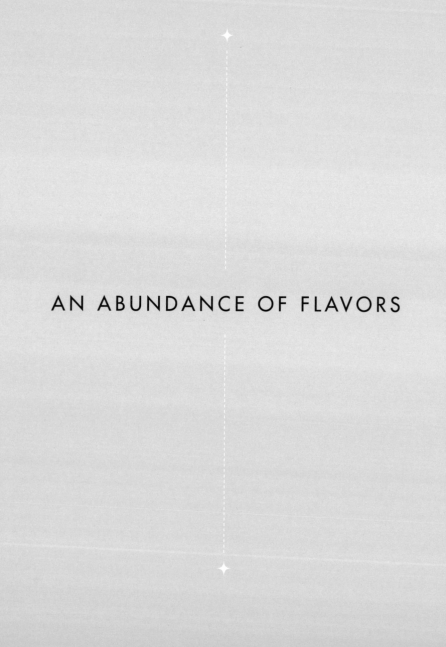

AN ABUNDANCE OF FLAVORS

GLIMMER ENVIRONMENTS

LET A JOY KEEP YOU. REACH OUT YOUR HANDS
AND TAKE IT WHEN IT RUNS BY.

— CARL SANDBURG

When we find a glimmer, we are naturally pulled to return to where we found it and look for another. The places in the world where we regularly find glimmers become our glimmer environments. For each of us, some places are more apt to hold glimmers than others, and when we discover the themes, we can find glimmer-filled environments wherever we go. When we see where our predictable glimmer moments occur, we can craft a routine that takes us to those places.

DISCOVER EVERYDAY
GLIMMER PLACES

As we navigate our everyday lives, we often move through the same places on a regular basis. Some of these everyday places predictably bring us glimmers.

NOTICE WHERE YOU ARE WHEN YOU FIND A GLIMMER.

RETURN TO A PLACE WHERE YOU FOUND A
GLIMMER AND LOOK FOR ANOTHER ONE.

WHERE DO YOU FIND GLIMMERS
IN BUILT ENVIRONMENTS?

WHERE DO YOU FIND GLIMMERS IN
THE NATURAL ENVIRONMENT?

WHAT ARE THE QUALITIES OF THE PLACES THAT
CALL TO YOU AND BRING YOU GLIMMERS?

DISCOVER THE PLACES THAT BRING YOU GLIMMERS . . .

FIND YOUR SOUL HOME

Certain places make us feel like we're being held in a stream of glimmers. When we find that place, we instinctively know we are safe. This is more than a place that welcomes us. This is a place that brings a deep sense of belonging—a place where our soul feels at home.

DISCOVER THE GEOGRAPHY THAT FEELS
ALIVE WITH GLIMMERS (E.G., THE SEA,
FOREST, MOUNTAINS, DESERT, PRAIRIE).
VISIT PLACES AND SEE WHERE YOU
INSTINCTIVELY FEEL AT HOME.
REMEMBER PLACES YOU'VE BEEN AND NOTICE THE
ONES THAT BROUGHT YOU A SENSE OF BELONGING.

RECOGNIZE YOUR SOUL HOME.

TAKE YOUR GLIMMERS
WITH YOU

While we may not always be able to return to our glimmer environment, we can take a reminder of it with us to touch into whenever we need a bit of glimmer energy.

FRAME A PHOTO OF YOUR GLIMMER ENVIRONMENT.

FIND OBJECTS THAT REMIND YOU OF
YOUR GLIMMER ENVIRONMENT.

PUT REMINDERS WHERE YOU SEE THEM.

CARRY A REMINDER WITH YOU.

COLLECT YOUR GLIMMER REMINDERS.

MY WORLD OF GLIMMERS

SHARING GLIMMERS

THOUSANDS OF CANDLES CAN BE LIGHTED FROM
A SINGLE CANDLE, AND THE LIFE OF THE CANDLE
WILL NOT BE SHORTENED. HAPPINESS NEVER
DECREASES BY BEING SHARED.

— THE BUDDHA

Co-regulation is an essential ingredient in well-being. It deepens our sense of caring and being cared about. First, finding and feeling glimmers brings micromoments of safety and shapes our systems in the direction of connection. Then, sharing our glimmers with others deepens the experience, bringing the moments alive again in the remembering and retelling. And finally, hearing someone else's glimmer experience invites us into their world and often lands as a glimmer for us too.

MAKE A GLIMMER
CONNECTION

A focus on sharing glimmers is a pathway to connection. We find common ground with others in ways that are uncomplicated and easy to enter into.

FIND A GLIMMER BUDDY.

FORM A GLIMMER GROUP.

START A WORKPLACE GLIMMER LIST CATALOGUE.

CREATE A NEIGHBORHOOD GLIMMER LIST.

INVITE GLIMMER CONNECTIONS . . .

DEVELOP GLIMMER-SHARING PRACTICES

The ways we share glimmers may be as varied as the people with whom we are sharing.

GO ON A GLIMMER WALK WITH A FRIEND.
TAKE A FRIEND WITH YOU TO YOUR GLIMMER
ENVIRONMENT. VISIT THEIR GLIMMER ENVIRONMENT.
SEND GLIMMER MESSAGES OR EMAILS.
CREATE A GLIMMER SHORTHAND USING EMOJIS.
SEND GLIMMER PHOTOS.

DISCOVER YOUR GLIMMER-SHARING PRACTICES . . .

THE JOY OF
SHARING GLIMMERS

GLIMMERING

NO ACT OF KINDNESS, NO MATTER HOW
SMALL, IS EVER WASTED.

— AESOP

Glimmers are good for us, good for others, and good for the world. When we find a glimmer, we feel the spark of goodness it brings. Glimmers shape our systems toward connection and take us on a path to personal well-being. Then, as we are able to anchor in regulation, we send glimmers out into the world and can be a glimmer for others. If we think about benevolence as the intentional use of our regulated presence in service of healing, then glimmering is a way to beam benevolence as we move through the world.

BE A GLIMMER IN SOMEONE'S DAY

As you move through your day, notice when you are feeling regulated and connected—remember, you can share that energy with the people around you.

OFFER A SMILE TO SOMEONE.

MAKE A GESTURE OF WELCOME.

SEND A HEART WITH YOUR HANDS.

WRITE A NOTE TO A FRIEND.

SAY SOMETHING NICE TO A STRANGER.

EXPLORE ALL THE WAYS YOU CAN BE A GLIMMER
FOR OTHERS . . .

EXPAND YOUR GLIMMERING

When you lend a helping hand to a group or organization, you are sharing your glimmer energy and the ripple effect of your glimmering helps shape that system. When you join with others to stand up for a cause and stay anchored in regulation, you send glimmers to everyone around you and can be a powerful force for goodness.

VOLUNTEER AT AN ORGANIZATION
THAT IS MEANINGFUL TO YOU.
DONATE TIME OR MONEY TO A CAUSE YOU BELIEVE IN.
JOIN A MARCH OR PROTEST.
SPEAK UP AGAINST INJUSTICE.

DISCOVER HOW YOUR GLIMMER PRESENCE IMPACTS
THE WORLD.

MY GLIMMERING MAKES A
DIFFERENCE

THE PATH FORWARD

THE GREATEST JOURNEY IS THE ONE OF
SELF-DISCOVERY.

— LAO TZU

As you reach the end of the *Glimmers Journal*, take time to reflect on your journey. You've traveled your own path to this ending. Along the way, you've recognized familiar glimmer experiences and discovered new ones. Finding and feeling the energy of glimmers has become a natural part of your day. You know where to reliably find glimmers and are ready for unexpected glimmer moments. Your *Glimmers Journal* is a resource you can return to. The glimmers you identified are documented in your journal and stored in your nervous system. You can revisit them and relive the moments at any time.

Your journal work may be completed, but finding glimmers and making new glimmer memories never ends. Glimmers are tiny moments that accumulate. They bring personal well-being and, like a stone dropped into the water, they send ripples out into the world. Gather your glimmers and nourish your nervous system. Help others find glimmers. Be a glimmering presence in the world.

RETURN ONCE MORE TO THE INTENTION-SETTING
PRACTICE FROM THE BEGINNING OF THE JOURNAL
AND SET AN INTENTION FOR GLIMMERING. WRITE
AN INTENTION TO NOURISH YOURSELF THROUGH
GLIMMERS, AND SEND GLIMMERS OUT INTO THE
WORLD.

May your days be filled with glimmers,
Deb

THE SCIENCE OF FEELING SAFE ENOUGH TO FALL IN LOVE WITH LIFE

The autonomic nervous system is at the heart of our lived experience. It influences the way we live, love, and work; it guides how we move through the world. The nervous system is the common denominator in our human family, designed to help us successfully navigate the challenges of daily living, ensuring we survive in moments of danger and thrive in times of safety. Polyvagal Theory, developed by renowned scientist Stephen Porges, offers a guide to the inner workings of the autonomic nervous system and a way to partner with our nervous system to navigate this unfamiliar territory. According to Polyvagal Theory, three organizing principles—neuroception, hierarchy, and co-regulation—form the foundation of understanding how our nervous systems work.

NEUROCEPTION

The stories about who we are and how the world works originate in our autonomic state, are sent through autonomic pathways from the body to the brain, and are then translated by the brain into the beliefs that guide our daily living. The mind narrates what the nervous system knows. Story follows state. Before the brain understands and makes meaning of an experience, the autonomic nervous system has assessed the situation and initiated a response. Coined by Polyvagal Theory developer Stephen Porges, *neuroception* describes how our autonomic nervous system takes in information. This inner, subconscious surveillance system gathers information through three pathways: inside, listening to what is happening in our internal organs; outside, scanning the environment; and between, sensing the connection to another nervous system. Through neuroception, we are continuously broadcasting and receiving messages of welcome and warning. In response to the information that we receive via neuro-ception, the autonomic nervous system makes moment-to-moment decisions about safety and survival, and we move from state to state along the autonomic hierarchy.

● HIERARCHY

The autonomic nervous system responds to sensations in the body and signals from the environment through three pathways of response. These pathways work in a specified order and respond to challenges in predictable ways called the autonomic hierarchy. Each pathway brings its own set of thoughts, feelings, behaviors, and bodily experiences. The three pathways (and their patterns of response), in evolutionary order from oldest to newest, are the dorsal vagus (immobilization), the sympathetic nervous system (mobilization), and the ventral vagus (social engagement and connection).

The ventral vagus, at the top of the autonomic hierarchy, is the system of connection. The ventral state is essential for health and well-being. In this state, we feel grounded, organized, and ready to meet the day. Life feels manageable; we see options, have hope, and hear new stories. We connect to ourselves, to others, to the world around us, and to Spirit. We are regulated and ready to engage.

The sympathetic system, down one step on the hierarchy, is a system of mobilization. In its everyday function, it helps regulate heart and breath rhythms and brings us energy to move through the day. In its survival role, it activates pathways of fight and flight and pulls us into anxiety and anger.

The dorsal mode, at the bottom of the hierarchy, in its everyday role regulates digestion, bringing nutrients to nourish us. When recruited in service of survival, dorsal becomes a system of shutting down. We feel drained, without enough energy to engage with the world. We collapse, disconnect, and disappear.

We regularly travel this hierarchy as we navigate the challenges of daily living. In fact, none of us are always anchored in regulation. That is an unreasonable and unachievable goal. Well-being comes from a nervous system that moves out of ventral regulation into sympathetic and dorsal dysregulation and finds the way back to ventral. Moving out of regulation into sympathetic or dorsal survival is not the problem. It is only when we move out of regulation and get stuck in survival that we suffer.

● CO-REGULATION

Co-regulation is necessary, first to survive and then to thrive. It is a biological imperative—a need that must be met to sustain life. Through reciprocal regulation of our autonomic states, we feel safe to move into connection and create trusting relationships. As we grow, we add the ability to self-regulate, but we never lose the need and the longing to be safely connected to others. Through co-regulation, a foundation of safety is created, and nourishing connections follow. Co-regulation creates a physiological platform of safety that supports a psychological story of security that then leads to social engagement. The autonomic nervous systems of two individuals find sanctuary in a co-created experience of connection. We live in a culture that encourages autonomy and independence, and yet we need to remember that we are wired to live in connection. Co-regulation is a necessary ingredient for physical and emotional well-being. Throughout our lives we look for, and long for, safe and reliable connections.

THE BEGINNER'S GUIDE TO
POLYVAGAL THEORY

Dr. Stephen Porges, originator of Polyvagal Theory, identified a biological order of human response that is active in all human experience. With gratitude to Dr. Porges for his work, this beginner's guide explores and explains Polyvagal Theory in user-friendly language.

We come into the world wired to connect. With our first breath, we embark on a lifelong quest to feel safe in our bodies, in our environments, and in our relationships with others. The autonomic nervous system is our personal surveillance system, always on guard, asking the question, "Is this safe?" Its goal is to protect us by sensing safety and risk, listening moment by moment to what is happening in and around our bodies and in the connections we have to others. This listening happens far below awareness and far away from our conscious control. Dr. Porges, understanding that this awareness does not come with conscious perception, coined the term *neuroception* to describe the way our autonomic nervous system scans for cues of safety, danger, and life threat without involving the thinking parts of our brain. Because we humans are meaning-making beings, what begins as the wordless experience of neuroception drives the creation of a story that shapes our daily living.

The autonomic nervous system is made up of two main branches, the sympathetic and the parasympathetic, and responds to signals and sensations via three pathways, each with a characteristic pattern of response. Through each of these pathways, we react in service of survival.

The sympathetic branch is found in the middle of the spinal cord and represents the pathway that prepares us for action. It responds to cues of danger and triggers the release of adrenaline, which fuels the fight-or-flight response.

Polyvagal Theory focuses on two pathways of the parasympathetic branch traveling within a nerve called the vagus. Vagus, meaning "wanderer," is aptly named. From the brain stem at the base of the skull, the vagus travels in two directions: downward through the lungs, heart, diaphragm, and stomach, and upward to connect with nerves in the neck, throat, eyes, and ears. The vagus is divided into two parts: the ventral vagal pathway and the dorsal vagal pathway. The ventral vagal pathway responds to cues of safety and supports feelings of being safely engaged and socially connected. In contrast, the dorsal vagal pathway responds to cues of extreme danger. It takes us out of connection, out of awareness, and into a protective state of collapse. When we feel collapsed, numb, or not present, the dorsal vagus has taken control.

Dr. Porges identified a hierarchy of response built into our autonomic nervous system and anchored in the evolutionary development of our species. The origin of the dorsal vagal pathway of the parasympathetic branch and its immobilization response lies with our ancient vertebrate ancestors, and it is the oldest pathway. The sympathetic branch and its pattern of mobilization was next to develop. The most recent addition, the ventral vagal pathway of the parasympathetic branch, brings patterns of social engagement that are unique to mammals.

When we are firmly grounded in our ventral vagal pathway, we feel safe and connected, calm and social. A sense (neuroception) of danger can trigger us out of this state and backward on the evolutionary timeline into the sympathetic branch. Here we are mobilized to respond and take action. Taking action can help us return to the safe and social state. It is when we feel as though we are trapped and can't escape danger that the dorsal vagal pathway pulls us all the way back to our evolutionary beginnings. In this state, we are immobilized. We shut down to survive. From here, it is a long way back to feeling safe and social and a painful path to follow.

THE AUTONOMIC LADDER

Let's translate our basic knowledge of the autonomic nervous system into everyday understanding by imagining the autonomic nervous system as a ladder. How do our experiences change as we move down and back up the ladder?

THE TOP OF THE LADDER

Safety and connection are guided by the evolutionarily newest part of the autonomic nervous system. Our social engagement system is active in the ventral vagal pathway of the parasympathetic branch. In this state, our heart rate is regulated, our breath full. We take in the faces of friends; we can tune in to conversations and tune out distracting noises. We see the big picture and connect to the world and the people in it. I might describe myself as happy, active, and, interested and the world as safe, fun, and peaceful. From this ventral vagal place at the top of the autonomic ladder, I am connected to myself and can reach out to others. Some of the daily living experiences of this state include being organized, following through with plans, taking care of myself, taking time to play, doing things with others, feeling productive at work, and having a general feeling of regulation and a sense of management. Health benefits include a healthy heart, regulated blood pressure, a healthy immune system decreasing my vulnerability to illness, good digestion, quality sleep, and an overall sense of well-being.

ONE STEP DOWN THE LADDER

The sympathetic branch of the autonomic nervous system activates when we feel a stirring of unease—when something triggers a neuroception of danger. We go into action. Fight or flight happens here. In this state, our heart rate speeds up, our breath is short and shallow, we scan our environment looking for danger—we are on the move. I might describe myself as anxious or angry and feel the rush of adrenaline that makes it hard for me to be still. I am listening for sounds of danger and don't hear the sounds of friendly voices. The world may feel dangerous, chaotic, and unfriendly. From this place of sympathetic mobilization—a step down the autonomic ladder and backward on the evolutionary timeline—I may believe that the world is a dangerous place and I need to protect myself from harm. Some of the daily living problems can be anxiety, anger, inability to focus or follow through, and distress in relationships. Health consequences can include heart disease; high blood pressure; high cholesterol; sleep problems; weight gain;

Ventral Vagal

Sympathetic

Dorsal Vagal

memory impairment; headache; chronic neck, shoulder, and back tension; stomach problems; and increased vulnerability to illness.

THE BOTTOM OF THE LADDER

Our oldest pathway of response, the dorsal vagal pathway of the parasympathetic branch, is the path of last resort. When all else fails, when we are trapped and taking action doesn't work, the primitive vagus takes us into shutdown, collapse, and dissociation. Here at the very bottom of the autonomic ladder, I am alone with my despair and escape into not knowing, not feeling, almost a sense of not being. I might describe myself as hopeless, abandoned, foggy, too tired to think or act, and the world as empty, dead, and dark. From this earliest place on the evolutionary timeline, where my mind and body have moved into conservation mode, I may believe that I am lost and no one will ever find me. Some of the daily living problems can be dissociation, problems with memory, depression, isolation, and no energy for the tasks of daily living. Health consequences of this state can include chronic fatigue, fibromyalgia, digestive issues, low blood pressure, and respiratory problems.

MOVING ON THE LADDER

Now that we've explored each of the places on the autonomic ladder, let's consider how we move up and down. Our preferred place is at the top of the ladder. The ventral vagal state is hopeful and resourceful. We can live, love, and laugh by ourselves and with others. This is not a place where everything is wonderful or a place without problems. But it is a place where we have the ability to acknowledge distress and explore options, to reach out for support and develop organized responses. We move down the ladder into action when we are triggered into a sense of unease—of impending danger. We hope that taking action here will give us enough space to take a breath and climb back up the ladder to the place of safety and connection. It is when we fall all the way down to the bottom rungs that the safety and hope at the top of the ladder feel unreachable.

SYSTEMS WORKING TOGETHER

We experience well-being when the three parts of our autonomic nervous system work together. To understand this integration, we leave the imagery of the ladder and imagine instead a home. The dorsal vagal system runs the basic utilities of the home. This system works continually in the background, keeping our basic body systems online and in order. When there is a glitch in the system, we pay attention. When all is running smoothly, the body's functions work automatically. Without the influence of the ventral vagal system, the basic utilities run the empty house, but no one is home. Or, if we are home, the environment is one that brings no comfort. Everything is turned down to the lowest possible setting—enough to keep the air circulating and the pipes from freezing. The environment is just habitable enough to sustain life. The sympathetic branch can be thought of as the home security system maintaining a range of responses and armed to react to any emergencies. This alarm system is designed to trigger an immediate response and then return to standby. Without the influence of the ventral vagal system, the alarm system receives a steady stream of emergency notifications and continues to sound the alarm. The ventral vagal system allows us to soak in, and savor, this home we are inhabiting. We can enjoy it as a place to rest and renew by ourselves and as a place to join with friends and family. We feel the basic utilities running in the background. The rhythms of our heart and breath are regulated. We trust that the monitoring system is on standby. The integration of systems allows us to be compassionate, curious about the world we live in, and emotionally and physically connected to the people around us.

This beginner's guide is written to offer an understanding of the autonomic nervous system's role and responses in service of our safety and survival. With this knowledge, we can begin to befriend the autonomic nervous system and map our personal response patterns. The befriending skills lead to attending practices. Our mapping leads naturally to tracking. With the awareness of tracking, we can begin to intentionally tune and tone our autonomic nervous system. We can successfully navigate our quest for safety and connection.

ACKNOWLEDGMENTS

This past year has been a time of challenges and changes. There have been personal moments of distress along with global events that have shaped my stories of safety and connection and impacted the way I live, love, and work. It's been hard to hold on to regulation, and many times I've found myself in moments of messiness. Working on the *Glimmers Journal* has been a testament to how glimmers can be a lifeline in times of great challenge. My husband, Bob, died in September 2023, and glimmers kept me going when the weight of grief threatened to overwhelm me. Creating the *Glimmers Journal* was a godsend, helping me navigate my days with some semblance of grace. As I write these acknowledgments, I think about Stephen Porges and the many glimmers he has brought to my life. Without Steve's brilliant work, my work would not be possible. And without his kindness and friendship, my life would be so much less joyful. Tina, Marilyn, and Linda have unfailingly walked with me over the past months both in person and virtually, letting me know I'm not alone and giving me space to find my way. Somehow they always knew just what was needed. My daughters, Katy and Ann, have been by my side helping me learn to navigate life without Bob. I love collecting glimmers with them and making new memories.

I usually write in solitude but writing the *Glimmers Journal* felt like a shared effort. My daughters, my grandchildren, and even my daughter's friends sent me glimmers when I needed inspiration, and I'm sure they'll recognize some of their suggestions in the journal pages. I'm grateful to all my dear friends who reached out to share a glimmer. Each time I was reminded that I am not alone. People I've never met regularly shared their glimmer moments with me through email, which was a surprise and a delight. My wonderful editor, Deborah Malmud, believed in this project from the beginning and was always there to guide me. She is not only an expert editor but a wise and kind human, and I feel blessed that she is a part of my life. Deborah and her team at Norton reassured me that whenever I was ready to send the journal pages, they would be there to receive them. It is their expertise that turns words on a page into beautiful books.

I am touched by all the ways glimmers bring people together. Writing the *Glimmers Journal* has helped me deepen my own practice and made me even more passionate about helping people discover the power of glimmers. Sending gratitude to each of you for being a part of my world and a glimmer to light your way . . .

ABOUT THE AUTHOR

Deb Dana, LCSW, is a clinician, consultant, author, and speaker. Her work is focused on using the lens of Polyvagal Theory to understand and resolve the impact of trauma and creating ways of working that honor the role of the autonomic nervous system. She delves into the intricacies of how understanding and befriending our own nervous systems can change the way we navigate our daily lives. Deb is well known for translating Polyvagal Theory into a language and application that is both clear and accessible and for her significant contribution pioneering Rhythm of Regulation® methodology, tools, techniques, and practices which continue to open up the power of Polyvagal Theory for professionals and curious people from diverse backgrounds and all walks of life. Deb can be contacted via her website www.rhythmofregulation.com.